Content Streaming and Digital Media Solutions:

The Past, Present, and Future with Practical Applications for the Business World

A Handy and Practical Reference Guide for using Video, Content Streaming, Webcasting and all things digital for your Marketing, CorpComm, Training, PR, IR and communications needs.

Scott Kutos

Introduction

Content Streaming as a component of Digital Media Solutions (DMS) has been available now for more than twenty years. But what is it, and why is it still regarded by many as magic? We will attempt to answer these and other questions in our search to unravel this mystery and bring Content Streaming to the forefront of your everyday business practices as we move into the third decade of the twenty-first century.

So what is Content Streaming? Content Streaming refers to the ability to share real-time audio and/or video and other applications across the Internet, either internal to the network or externally to your customers or the general public. Most people will immediately think of a YouTube application, but Content Streaming is much more than that. Content Streaming *can* refer to video sharing in one of its simpler forms. We will attempt to describe the myriad terms that make up a company's Digital Media Solutions offering by answering the following questions:

- What is a Digital Media Solution and where does Content Streaming fit in?

- Why do I need to use Content Streaming?
- When should I use Content Streaming?
- How best do I use Content Streaming in my daily business practices?
- What are the benefits and 'best fit' for my Content Streaming/Digital Media Solutions strategy?

By the time you are through with this study we hope you will understand the importance and benefits of a Digital Media Strategy in your everyday business practice, along with the vital role Content Streaming fits into this strategy. You will easily understand the ROI (Return on Investment) brought about by your Digital Media Solutions strategy, and you will become an expert in Content Streaming. You will no longer see Content Streaming as magic; rather, you will understand the importance of this technology not only in communicating with your customers but how it can enhance revenue and reduce costs for your firms' Marketing, Training, and Corporate Communications verticals.

Definitions

Before we start on our exploration of Content Streaming, let's first begin with the basics of Digital Media Solutions and definitions of terms.

Digital Media Solutions – This refers to any form of digital communication used in the modern workplace. Communications can be internal (inside the corporation), external (marketing, investor relations, Social Media, etc.) or both.

Content Streaming – Content Streaming is a term used to describe the sharing of any digital content over the Internet. This content can be digital audio, digital video, collateral (PDF, Word, MS applications, GIFs, etc.), or any combination of these. The Streaming may be Live (real-time Stream with a virtual live audience), on-demand (the Stream is viewed at a time deemed suitable by the end viewer), or Simulive (digital content is pre-recorded then streamed live at a set time).

Enterprise – this term refers to the entire infrastructure of a company as relates to your digital strategy. From a business standpoint this can also refer to knowledge workers inside an organization. The Enterprise for an automobile manufacturer, for example, would include all of the knowledge workers scattered throughout the company but would *not* include line workers on the factory floor (since they typically are not considered knowledge workers and would not typically take part in the development and sharing of Content Streaming). Enterprises can range from one hundred to over one hundred thousand.

Content Delivery Network - (CDN) The Content Delivery Network is the platform on which your content will Stream across the Internet. Companies such as Akamai, BlueCoat and others serve as transport companies to carry your digital stream across the Internet using Routers and Edge Routers to transmit, direct, and guide the stream to a specific ending destination or destinations.

Virtual Private Network – (VPN) A VPN serves as the internal digital infrastructure for your company's enterprise. The VPN is a software application that allows for communications internal to the company firewall in a secure framework protected by the Firewall.

Firewall - The Firewall is a software application installed by your company's IT department to prevent outside intrusion into your enterprise VPN. The main purpose of the Firewall is to provide security from deliberate attack by an entity residing outside your enterprise.

<u>Enterprise Content Delivery Network</u> – (eCDN) The eCDN is a relatively recent tool developed to ease the burden of transmitting huge amounts of data through the VPN of a company's Enterprise. We will discuss this in much greater detail later on in the book. Companies such as Kollective, Kaltura, Ramp, Vbrick, and Hive have developed eCDNs to work with your Content Streaming application and provide bandwidth mitigation to ease the demand on your enterprise network.

<u>Unicast Streaming</u> – Unicast Streaming is the original form of Content Streaming. In a Unicast environment the digital stream is sent out from the source to every participant attaching to

the Stream, and individually. This is the most bandwidth-intensive form of streaming: If you are streaming live to thousands of end users (participants), your Stream will be copied thousands of time and to each individual end user. If a single Stream of video content uses 300kbps of bandwidth, then unicast streams to thousands of end users will take millions or billions of kbps bandwidth to support. Your VPN will most likely crash!

Multicast Streaming – unlike Unicast Streaming Multicast streaming lumps all of your end users (participants) of a live Stream into one single Stream. The Multicast Stream will amalgamate all of the end users into one single stream as it leaves your network, only breaking up into individual streams when it is picked up by individual end users. This saves a tremendous amount of bandwidth for your enterprise VPN.

Bandwidth — Bandwidth is a term used by all IT departments to define the amount of memory being used in Content Streaming. Bandwidth is typically defined in kbps (kilobytes per second) and as a percentage of the entire bandwidth available to a company's VPN. Typical bandwidth used for a Unicast Stream for audio content is 50kbps. Typical bandwidth used for a Unicast Stream for video content is 300kbps. If the enterprise — theoretically — only has 300meg available for Streaming, as the Unicast bandwidth approaches 50% capacity the stream will begin to buffer or completely stop for the end user (not to mention your IT staff will be forced to shut other non-vital systems down as the bandwidth for your stream eventually takes up the majority of bandwidth available. This will result in extremely aggressive emails from your IT staff!).

There are many more definitions in regards to Digital Media Solutions and Content Streaming, but the outline above will give you a good, fundamental understanding of some of the terminology needed as we move forward in our exploration of DMS. I will be sure to define any new terms introduced throughout this book clearly and precisely leaving no doubt as to where these fit in to your digital strategy.

<u>Adobe Flash</u> - Adobe Flash is a multimedia software platform used for production of animations, rich Internet applications, desktop applications, and embedded web browser video players. Flash is (or was...) extensively used for producing graphics animations.

<u>RTMP</u> – Real-Time Messaging Protocol. RTMP was developed as a protocol for streaming audio, video and other data over the Internet between a Flash player and a server. RTMP is the supporting protocol on which Flash Content Streaming is delivered over the Internet.

HTML5 – Hypertext Markup Language revision 5 (HTML5) is the markup language for the structure and presentation of World Wide Web (internet) contents. HTML5 supports the traditional HTML syntax and other new features in its markup, new APIs, and error handling. It is the solution of choice for mobile applications and Content Streaming.

HLS – HTTP Live Streaming. HLS was developed by Apple as a media streaming communications protocol for delivering HTML5 applications over the Internet. It has been widely adopted for use on all platforms providing Content Streaming applications over the Internet. HLS is the equivalent of RTMP:

RTMP is the supporting protocol on which HTML5 Content Streaming is delivered over the Internet. Unlike RTMP, HLS *does* support mobile applications. It is currently the only protocol supporting Content Streaming to mobile devices.

Webcast – A webcast is a media presentation distributed over the Internet using Streaming Media Technology to distribute a single-content source to many simultaneous listeners or viewers. Essentially, "webcasting" is broadcasting over the Internet. Synonyms: Webinar, Streaming

Content Streaming – History

It was a cold, dark day in the world of Digital Media some twenty years ago, when suddenly Adobe created a software solution to be known as Flash. Flash! What a great name! It immediately conjured up excitement in the world of Digital Media, so much so that all of the Content Streaming solutions came to use it as the basis for streaming across the Internet.

Flash, by definition, is a deprecated multimedia software platform used for production of animations, rich Internet applications, desktop applications, mobile applications (though this is up for debate...), games and web browser video players (per Wikipedia). For the layman, this means we now had the ability to stream rich media applications in real time. Custom GIFs (Graphic Interchange Format) were created that allowed logos to dance and change form on our screen. The world suddenly realized they could use an Adobe Flash Player to stream audio and video files across the Internet easily and effortlessly. Applications such as YouTube, Vimeo and Webcasting (Streaming and Webinars) became household names.

How does Flash work? Flash, again, is a software program that uses RTMP (Real-Time

Messaging Protocol) to allow the transmission of video files across the Internet - or your VPN or your Intranet - and in real time. RTMP was created by a company called Macromedia, soon to be purchased by Adobe. So the marriage of RTMP with Flash was inevitable.

Adobe Flash has dominated the Streaming market now for more than 20 years. Basically, for a webcasting application, all of the files, stream, etc., are converted to Flash format before being released to the Internet for a live (or on-demand) event. This allows the seamless viewing of the files by the end user or participant in the event. There are two downsides, however. Files converted to Flash have no way of being converted back to their original format. So, if you are using a PowerPoint file for your webcast event, your participants can't simply download the file from the Flash player. You would have to send out a link to the participants to the originally formatted file in order for your audience to download and save to their local device.

The second issue with Flash (and, therefore, video) is bandwidth. Flash files and video files are bandwidth hogs! A single unicast stream using RTMP and Flash for streaming video can use up to 300kbps of bandwidth. This is fine if you are the only person viewing, but if you try to open another application while viewing the stream you will most likely experience buffering or even signal outage or stream stoppage because your endpoint can't allocate the bandwidth to both the stream and your new application successfully.

And it gets even worse! If you are on a live broadcast from inside your corporate VPN trying to view your CEO on video, chances are your bandwidth consumption will max out the availability across the VPN, assuming you aren't the only one viewing the CEO's speech. That's when IT departments get testy and threaten to take away your Internet privileges. We'll talk more about this in a later chapter (see eCDN).

So what was happening during the early days of Content Streaming? How was this new-fangled technology used?

Near the end of the 20th century Content Streaming was typically hosted as an on-demand application. Intel chips just couldn't handle the bandwidth required for large-scale live Streaming. Facebook was not yet created, and while YouTube was popular, it was not being used for true workforce applications (kittens falling off of table-tops were the mainstream media at the time...). Content creators would use on-demand applications for advertising and product information dissemination.

In the mid-2000s I joined a small, startup Streaming company in Washington, DC. The company had a rollercoaster history, but I was intrigued by the technology and having just come from another technology company it seemed like a natural fit. Our customers were both commercial and Federal. We did a lot of work for companies like National Geographic, the Heritage Foundation, the National Association of Realtors, and communications companies like SciMed, Synaps, Visual Alchemy, FleishmanHillard, and many others. Our Federal customers included FDIC,

Department of Defense, Department of Commerce, even the State Department and Department of the Interior. We had a unique position in Washington, being close to the departments that needed outreach via the Web to constituents, and close enough to the advertising mecca in New York City to work with these large advertising and communications companies. I was heading up sales for this startup, working closely with the President of the company and Vice President of Operations to provide the best solution for the customers' needs. We employed a team of Streaming Media Content Developers who would take the various files presented by the client (video clips, PDFs, bios, PowerPoint files, etc.) and turn them into dynamic Web Streaming applications. We created thousands of hours of rich content for our customers. Customers such as National Geographic used us to transform wildlife videos into rich, graphics supported webcasts for their website: info-tainment, if you will. Communications companies used our services for getting information from pharmaceutical companies into the browsers of the population. We created advertisements for dozens of different products, all using canned (B-roll) video clips of doctors hyping the product along with a PowerPoint outlining the benefits of the offering. The Federal Government used our solutions to provide both internal and public facing content portals. Webcasts were created and hosted on department Intranet sites for employee information. On-demand video webcasts were made available to the public to outline the latest legislation passed by congress.

It was a great time to be in the Content Streaming business. And then Hurricane Katrina hit.

And our business took off even more...

The economy went into a bit of a recession as businesses halted travel.

Executives looked for ways to communicate virtually, and the live webcast came into its own.

Live webcasting had been around for some time, actually. Pharmaceutical companies especially loved it. They realized early on in the twenty-first century that getting an actual physician on camera was the best way to build up interest in a new drug. Companies like Pfizer, BMS, Merck and many others would spend tens of thousands of dollars on these live broadcasts. Since these were live events being streamed to the public, no one worried about bandwidth consumption. The idea was to broadcast a dinner meeting with a specific doctor or specialist who would endorse the company's products. We would bring in two- and three-camera crews to capture this. Of course, with doctors being so busy during the work day, these events were streamed live during the evening. Also, we knew there would be a much more receptive and available audience in the evening to view these live events.

Another new live application that came popular at this time was the live town-hall event. Town halls are a great way to get information from subject matter experts into the hands of the masses. The masses could be the general public, a specific voting bloc for whom you are targeting, or the employees of the company. Just like the doctor dinners outlined above, we would bring in two- and three-camera crews along with a Streaming technician to capture the video signal and Stream it across the Internet. Again, since these were public events, we never had to worry about bandwidth consumption. We completed town halls for the Heritage foundation, for the Federal Government, Catholic Charities, AARP, and many, many more.

But town halls for corporations and their enterprise weren't so easy. Connecting the video and audio streams to the Internet wasn't the issue: bandwidth was the issue. We could set up a three-camera shoot quickly and relatively easily. We would bring in the crew, set up the acoustics, including mics, monitors, even teleprompters. All we needed was a few hours of setup and testing, and we were ready to broadcast. But if the town hall was to be streamed internally to the customer's network, we had issues. The eCDN hadn't been invented yet (more on that later), and Intel chips just didn't allow for enough bandwidth to have up to 300kpbs per end point to access the video stream without bringing down the VPN. IT staff hated us, even though we were bringing the CEO to their employees in real time. More often than not we had to request employees to squeeze into auditoriums, conference rooms and to share endpoints in order to minimize bandwidth. We would alert employees working remotely to NOT log onto the corporate VPN in order to free up bandwidth. Many times we simply had to dumb down the broadcast from video and PowerPoint to simple audio. It was frustrating for both the customer and us as the service provider.

Streaming to the world was becoming commonplace, however. And we had many customers that used this new technology to broadcast important events to the world. One that comes to mind was the grand opening of the Royal Saudi University in Riyadh, Saudi Arabia. We got the request for this service from one of our strategic partners. The King of Saudi Arabia was opening the Royal Saudi University and wanted to share the event with the world.

The beauty of Content Streaming is it is geographically agnostic. As long as we have a connection to the Internet we can stream to the world. All the end user needs is a web browser and access to the Internet. The King of Saudi Arabia wanted to announce the opening of the University in style. We arranged for a three-camera switch shoot on site in Riyadh. This means we had three professional cameras broadcasting the event live. We were able to connect with a local AV company in Riyadh, but we also had to get a Streaming tech on-site in Saudi Arabia. This was difficult, but not impossible. Once this was set, the next step was to arrange for closed captioning during the live broadcast. This was a bit trickier as we had to locate an Arabic speaking interpreter that would be on site and live in Washington, DC while the broadcast went live in Riyadh. The Stream went live at 8pm EDT with the interpreter on site, listening to the broadcast, then entering the Arabic into a laptop and transmitting that text in to our captioner remote in Maryland. The captioner then streamed the captions back to us in Arabic and English. The delay from the live event in Riyadh was about 45-60 seconds, so we were able to provide the closed captioning with little delay to the viewing audience. The whole event lasted about 90 minutes and went off without a hitch. The live viewing audience, unfortunately, was small, but the King didn't seem to mind. All he wanted to do was get the video of the opening ceremony streamed to the world, and we were able to execute that quite efficiently.

Another live town hall that stands out is the very first live Stream of a US President. It was spring, 2009. President Obama had only been in office for a few months when the National Academies of Science asked him to speak at their annual meeting. We won this business with an AV partner and quickly went about setting up the two-camera shoot. Since we were streaming from the nation's capital and the event was to be broadcast world-wide in real time we arranged for a satellite truck to be brought in for the Stream, rather than simply downloading the Stream to a T1 data line and directly to the Internet. This is a bit complex as we had to arrange for security clearances for all involved, from the crew on the ground to any remote personnel involved in handling the Stream. Satellite trucks can be expensive as they're typically rented for the entire day, regardless of actual broadcast time. But NAS felt it was worth the cost in order to ensure the Stream had no signal or bandwidth issues.

The event went off without issue. We tested the signal a few hours before President Obama was to go on stage, taking the audio and video signals from the camera crew, processing through our Flash Video Encoding software, and then streamed out to the satellite truck. At 11am the signal was given that the event was about to start, and we had to all go to our dedicated, secure locations once the event began. President Obama came out on stage and gave his speech to the audience at NAS, we captured the audio and video, and transmitted the signal to the waiting satellite truck which then beam the signal to the satellite network and out to the Internet. We had no issues with bandwidth or signal degradation because we were not streaming inside a customer network. We were all extremely pleased and proud to have been the first crew to Stream the President of the United States and live.

But we were getting more and more interest in live webcasts. On-demand webcasts were great, but the new norm was a live broadcast either to introduce training or marketing to the world. But as long as bandwidth was an issue inside the customer network we would have issues completing and competing with other forms of communication.

The here and now: advances in Streaming Technology

At long last, technology caught up to the issues plaguing the live Streaming application. The eCDN was born. eCDN stands for enterprise Content Delivery Network (see definitions above). As customers demanded more and more live events and streamed internal to their network, a solution had to be developed that could handle the issues of carrying a 300kbps stream to every user inside the customer network.

Here's how the eCDN works. As we outlined above, the big issue in the early days of Streaming was Bandwidth. Chipmakers didn't (and still don't) have the ability to handle the bandwidth needed to stream large files (video!) through the enterprise VPN. Users of a streaming service, attempting to stream video, had their participants experience buffering or even outages when attempting to view the files. So, while IT managers waited for the chip manufacturers to create a hardware solution, others went out and created the eCDN. The eCDN allows for simulation of multicast streaming in and through the enterprise VPN while minimizing bandwidth requirements.

Typical streaming application without an eCDN:

Typical Streaming application with a software-enabled eCDN:

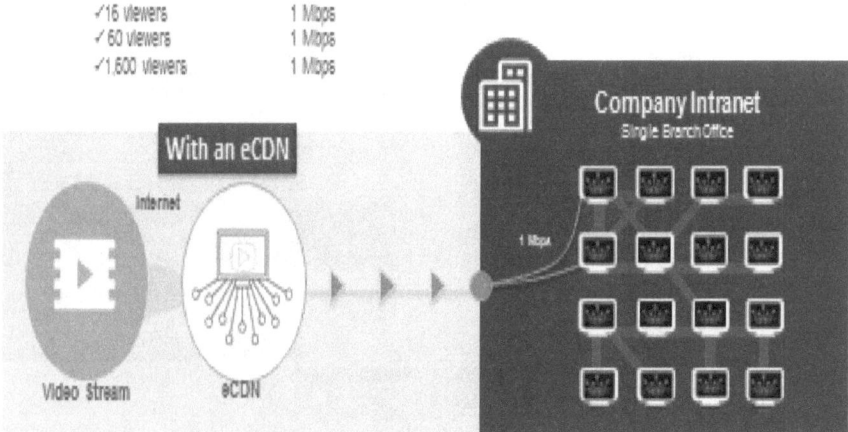

There are two basic methods of implementing an eCDN. The first is a pure software approach. Companies like Kollective, Kaltura and Hive have created a software app that is downloaded directly onto the end-user work station, inside the enterprise VPN, and acts to distribute the incoming Stream. The solution is known in the industry as a peering solution or software-defined solution. The app remains dormant until a Stream is detected at the enterprise level. The end-user doesn't even know the app is there and residing on their machine. Once activated, the app simply passes on the stream to the next work station in the enterprise. There is no limit to the number of 'hops' that can take place inside the eCDN. When the Stream enters the VPN, it engages the first work station on the enterprise. There is nothing special about that work station: it just happens to be the first work station encountered by the stream. The eCDN on that machine recognizes the stream, activates the eCDN app, and passes the stream on to the next work station in the network. This is known as peering. Again, there is no limit to the number of machines on the VPN. As long as the next machine in the chain has the eCDN app installed it will pick up the Stream and pass it on to the next. Very simple, very efficient.

But the solution does have some drawbacks. It is not what you might expect, however. There is no single point of failure in the solution. When one machine goes off line or fails, the solution simply drops that connection and the eCDN software continues unabated. Even if the point-of-entry machine goes off line, the solution is smart enough to move the next machine in the network to the entry point. No issues. The issue that does occur is delay. There is an average lag time between signal initiation to dispersion across the network of 20-30 seconds. This is, of course, invisible to the participant. The video and audio are in perfect sync, as long as the end user is using

VoIP to listen to the Stream. The delay can be a real problem, however, if anyone is listening to the broadcast using a phone line. The delay in the voice signal over a phone line, as we all know, is typically milliseconds. But this is excruciatingly painful when viewing the video stream that is delayed 30 seconds from the audio. Personally, I always encourage my customers NOT to use phone lines (except for the speaker). The delay issue is just too overpowering to overcome, and that typically means my customers are irate with me and my encoding team. Again, if the end users use VoIP, there is no delay between audio and video.

The second issue with the delay is that the Presenter must recognize this delay. If they push a poll or ask for feedback through a Q&A feature, then they must recognize that it will take at least 30 seconds for the feedback to come into their machine. It is advisable to conduct a dry run with speakers before the event goes live in order to acclimate the Speakers to the delay they will encounter on the live broadcast.

The third issue with the software enabled eCDN is security. In reality, this is more an issue of perception. Like all software solutions, there will be updates required in order to keep the installed apps current and up-to-date. In order to do this, the solution needs access to the Cloud. The Provider will have to work with the IT staff of the customer to gain access to the Firewall in order to install the solution as well as provide periodic updates. This is where the perceived security issues come into play. Most customers are fine with this. However, high-security customers like banks and financial institutions will not allow this. Personally, I've worked with several customers who simply refused to entertain the idea of a Cloud-supported software defined eCDN because of this perceived issue. I personally know of no known issues where a customer enterprise network has been compromised by an installed software eCDN, but the perception is out there and for high-security institutions this issue is real.

Software-enabled eCDNs are typically priced as a solution. The customer simply gives the provider the number of end users (or seats) required to be enabled (to have the app installed at the machine level), the level of support needed, and the provider works with the customer IT department to install the solution. Variables in pricing include support for on-demand videos (more on that later...) and the level of technical support needed. A typical install for an enterprise of 10,000 endpoints can run from $50k - $150k per year, depending on the variable requirements

imposed by the customer.

There is an answer to the perceived security issues regarding the Cloud and eCDN providers. This solution is a hardware-based eCDN. These are provided by vendors such as Ramp and Cisco/Vbrick.

Typical Streaming application with a hardware-enabled eCDN:

Hardware Defined eCDN

The Hardware Defined eCDN is set up behind your enterprise firewall/inside your VPN. This gives maximum security to video and content coming into your network.

Servers are set up to receive content, cache it (store it), then disseminate it through your network, either using Edge-Caching or a Multicast stream.

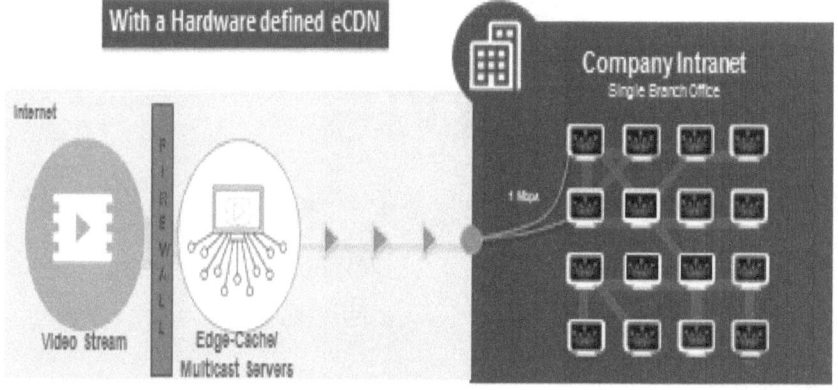

The primary difference, as can be seen, is that the hardware-enabled eCDN resides behind the customer's firewall and inside the enterprise VPN. This means that security is never compromised. The vendor never has to access the Cloud in order to either install the solution or update any software. The solution is installed completely by the customer's firewall, and any software updates are done by updating the software installed on the server rather than going through ports on the customer's firewall. This results in a very secure eCDN, and security conscious customers like financial institutions love this.

There are many variations of a hardware-enabled eCDN, but all work about the same way as I described above. Vendors typically allow customers to rent the servers required to operate the eCDN, so customers aren't forced to purchase both the server and any software required. The solution is sold in a similar manner as a software-defined eCDN: by subscription. The customer provides the number of knowledge workers (users) needed for the install, the vendor determines the number of servers required to support the install base, and the price of the annual subscription is generated to the customer. Pricing for this solution can run the gamut: I've seen installed subscriptions for as low as $6k per year to multiple hundreds of thousands of dollars. The price will depend not only on the enterprise install base but the type of solution required.

Options with a hardware-enabled eCDN Include:

Edge-Caching:

Servers Cache (store) video

No Desktop Install

Supports Mobile

Supports Live/On-Demand

Large impact on your LAN/VPN

Multicasting:

Server converts feed to Multicast Stream

Requires Desktop (software) Install

Does NOT support Mobile

Supports LIVE only

Minimal impact on your LAN/VPN

+++++

So we now have solved our video bandwidth dilemma. What is next? There have been many advances in Streaming technology and the means to provide the solution to the end user. Let's review these now.

Video

When I first got into the Streaming business video was for on-demand applications only. For live Content Streaming applications, more than 95% of these were audio-based. Any video applications were either on-demand (pre-recorded) or live for the purposes of streaming marketing events to the world. Customers like AARP and the Heritage foundation used our solutions to provide live video updates to their members: as long as these members were outside of their network and didn't take up internal bandwidth! Once the Stream left the source (inside the customer network) and was received by the end user the customer didn't care how much bandwidth it took up since it was only being received outside their network. But with the advancement of the eCDN, internal video communications became very much a reality. Customers like JPMorgan,

Fidelity Investments, IBM, Oracle and many others used video to communicate both internally and externally.

Video is now becoming the norm for live Streaming communications. Ten years ago, as I related above, the ratio of video communications to audio Streaming was less than 1:20. Today it is about 1:1. Video is becoming a ubiquitous component of the modern enterprise communications offering. Customers are now using video for town hall applications. It is now easy to get your CEO on camera for a Stream to the entire enterprise. The typical Webcasting application incorporates live video with a PowerPoint slide deck, polling, Q&A, even blogging and social media applications. In previous years, and in order for the entire enterprise to view the CEO address, management staff would herd all of the on-site employees into an auditorium for the event. Now, with an installed eCDN, there is no need (though this is still quite common: CEOs love to see her/his staff live so they can field live Q&A). It's become so ingrained into our everyday business practices that customers like Wells Fargo require video for all internal and external communications (see On-Demand Video Accessibility, to follow).

With a video and PowerPoint slides webcast the customer now has the power to communicate effectively and efficiently both internally and externally. I'll talk about this more in-depth later during this book, but you now have the capability to communicate in real time both with your employees and your customers, using both on-demand and live video applications. Video can be pre-recorded then loaded into the Webcast and streamed live to your audience, with Q&A occurring after the pre-recorded session is complete (we call this Simulive). Even Investor relations have gotten into the act: prior to 2015 almost all IR events were done by audio conference calls. Today the Streaming application allows for a cheaper and more effective communications method with your customer's entire board and shareholders. (IR departments are still video-shy, however. As of this writing it is still extremely rare for an IR event to use a video solution. Almost all employ either audio-only streaming or, at best, audio and PowerPoint slides.)

Video Hosting

Another Streaming tool that is coming into its own is Video Hosting. Vendors like Kaltura, Media Platform, and West all offer a video hosting application that attempts to mimic YouTube for the enterprise. These applications have been around for some time but are really just coming into their own in the enterprise video marketplace.

The first question that will come to your mind is, "if it's just like YouTube, why not just use YouTube?" The answers are many, but probably the most popular answer is security. YouTube does a great job of getting video to the masses, but it has no true security to limit access to videos by your competitors. In other words, there's no way to white-list (more on this later!) the access to the YouTube videos or even require registration to gain specific metrics on who is accessing and viewing your videos (more on this later, too!).

With a Video Hosting application you now have the ability to host all of your videos securely; even behind your firewall if you so desire. You have the ability to customize the viewing experience, allowing access to the entire enterprise or limiting the viewing to specific audiences. Once a hierarchy is determined and set up you will have the ability to host videos for specific departments, specific events, or even specific individuals. By setting up these parameters you are creating 'channels.' Video hosting channels, again, can be open to all within the enterprise, restricted by invitation only, or restricted by application (you must request access from the channel owner). Channel Owners are established, and he/she becomes the guardian of all the content within their specific channel. You can even create confidential and secret channels where the cannel isn't even visible to the enterprise; just the channel owner and selected team members. This is extremely effective for securing R&D videos or videos created by the executive team.

And video is not restricted to on-demand only. The Video Hosting application can also house live video Streams. Access to the live Stream can be open to the public or limited in the same manner as on-demand videos. These channels can even host live and on-demand Webcast events. By creating landing pages (again, more to follow), you can show a series of live and on-demand events for the viewing pleasure of your audience.

As you can probably surmise, this type of solution is entirely customizable. It may take 30-45 days to set the solution in place but once in place can be an extremely valuable asset. Like the eCDN solution, pricing is typically on a subscription basis with variable pricing set for the number of knowledge workers, the level of support required, and the customization required. Annual subscriptions, after the setup fee, can range from $50k to several hundred thousand dollars.

So what are the typical uses for a video hosting application? We will explore this further and later in the book, but I have customers that use video hosting for everything from on-boarding new employees to training to secure/top-secret video communications. There really is no limit to the applications. The customer can even make videos required viewing (for applications like HIPPA, EOE, etc.) with certifications and participation tracking. Training is probably the most popular application we've seen. On-demand training can be as simple as requiring the viewing of video to full certification with test scoring, grading and certification. Again, the capabilities of these platforms are almost unlimited, restricted only by the breadth and scope of the solution users and the budget necessary to implement.

To follow is a diagram of the flow of

Launch your own internal, secure video portal for training, knowledge sharing and corporate communications to deliver greater employee productivity and cost savings

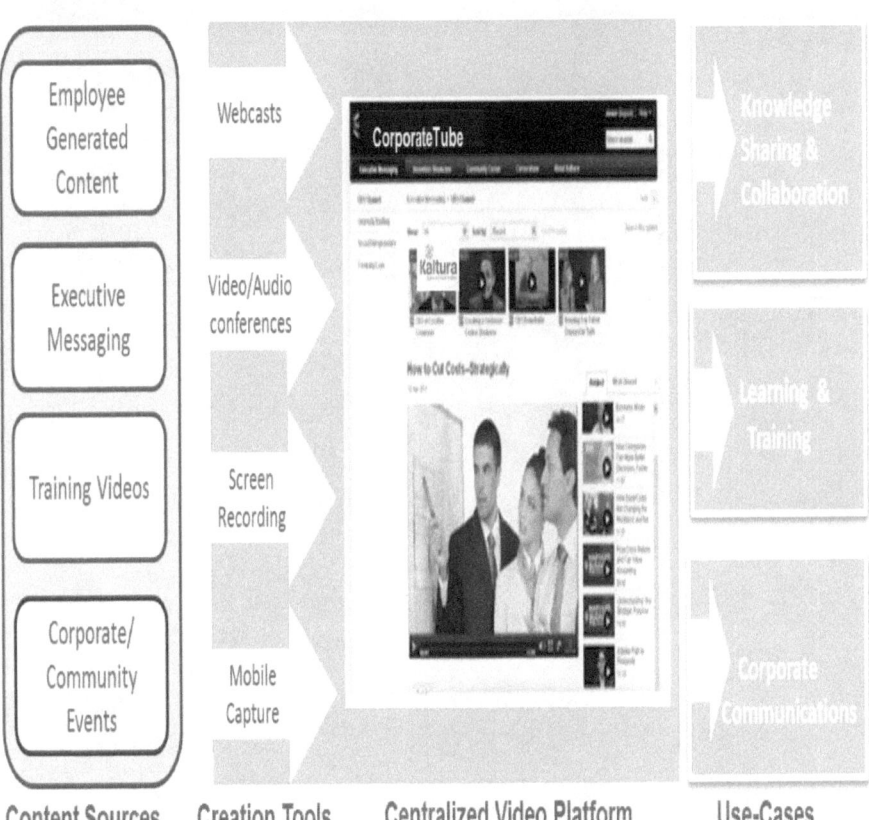

information (video!) through a Portal application:

Event Capture

Standard Streaming platforms offered by companies like On24, Arkaden, and West do a great job streaming to one virtual audience for short periods of time (by short, I mean two hours or less). But what can be done for larger events with multiple audiences or several topics to cover? The answer is Event Capture. Epiphan, a startup operation out of Palo Alto, CA, created a hardware and software Streaming application that allows for simultaneous capture of multiple live events. The Pearl box as offered by Epiphan can tie in two different Streams and split them out to multiple audiences, essentially allowing your live audience to pick and choose the event the wish to view. In fact, multiple Pearl boxes can be tied into the same webcasting Stream, thereby allowing unlimited breakout sessions during a live event. You now have the ability to host multiple training sessions or breakout sessions at the same time. Yes, it currently requires additional on-site Streaming technicians to manage this, but the Pearl is a breakthrough in getting your message out to your virtual audience.

There are several scenarios that could benefit from this technology. Probably the prime example is for large-scale conferences with multiple breakout sessions. A conference that occurs over multiple days would typically have multiple break-out sessions. The entire event can be captured on a Streaming platform with the breakout sessions happening live and made available to both your live and virtual audience. The virtual audience would register and log in for the main conference event, but once break-out sessions begin they would be offered the choice of joining any sub-session they prefer. The Pearl solution allows the viewer to participate in the break-out session then return to the main conference once the break-out session concludes. Price for renting the box and securing the live Streaming Technician is priced around $3,500 per day.

This technology is especially valuable for the on-demand session of the original live session. Once the live session is complete, the entire event is put up on the Internet as an on-demand playback. With registration the on-demand viewer is given the ability to pick and choose the sessions in which they want to participate. They can view any, all or none. And with the analytics available to the host we can capture that information and use that for future events and audiences (more on this later).

The Pearl solution from Epiphan has many other attributes. It allows the user to perform complex edits on a recorded solution, including adding graphics to enhance the viewing experience. It even allows for video splitting during the live event. This gives you the ability to stream the video of your panel while also viewing the questions being received from your live audience. The applications are myriad and quite diverse.

In-Room Mode

Speaking of the live, on-site audience, one of the newer applications to be added to our list of Streaming applications is called In-Room Mode. As the name implies, In-Room

Mode is an application made available only to the live (in-room) audience. With most live events there is an on-site audience as well as a virtual audience. This is typical of the town-hall application. Up until recently, the live audience could not participate in the Stream without having a mobile device to Stream the *entire* application while also attempting to view the live event.

In-Room Mode solves this dilemma. The live attendee can now bring a smartphone or tablet into the venue and log on to the event. While registering they are given the choice of logging in to the live Stream or logging in using In-Room Mode. Think of the In-Room Mode as a light version of the live Stream. Instead of presenting the entire webcast application to the viewer they are limited to the interactive features only. No live video, no live Streaming audio, no PowerPoint viewing. They do have the ability to submit questions and answer polls launched by the host during the live event. The idea is to keep the focus on the live speakers by limiting the distractions from the live Stream, and by limiting the interaction to question submission and poll answering the live audience member has essentially the same experience as the virtual participant.

Additionally, with a live town-hall application, once the preliminary presentation concludes the event turns to a Q&A session. By offering In-Room Mode to your live audience and questions submitted can be placed in queue during the presentation and transmitted to the presenter immediately upon conclusion of the presentation session. While the traditional Q&A session will most likely still occur with various team members walking through the audience with a hand-held microphone to capture questions the In-Room mode does this for you. It also allows for a better quality of questions since many live audience members will be reluctant to stand up in front of their peers and ask questions. And with the queuing capability of the live Stream the presenter or host will be able to screen questions in advance for relevance and suitability for the subject.

The In-Room application even allows for sharing of the event on social media, should the event host allow this. But more on this later...

The Registration Page (Landing Page)

The first element your streaming provider will create for your event is the landing page. This is a web application that serves as the initial contact to your audience. The landing page is important for several reasons. Again, it serves as the introductory link to your company and your event. It also houses the registration function which will be used to set up the database for your event and house all of the data you capture on your audience. More on this later.

The URL for the landing page is typically provided to your target audience through a link in an email blasted out by your firm. This can be the URL created by your streaming provider and will look something like this:

https://eventstream.com/IBDwe2/ID=23ip7user

…not very sexy. But perfectly acceptable for your internal applications. If you have an external event, such as a marketing webcast, you can disguise the URL so it is more user-friendly and subjective of the actual event:

[Click here to register for our marketing seminar](#)

    The breadth and scope of effort put into your landing page should be determined by the audience that will be accessing it. If you are doing an internal town hall you don't need to put much effort into your landing page, since you expect your employees to attend and don't want to spend the effort making a glamorous landing page. However, if you are creating a webcast to market a new pharmaceutical drug to the medical industry, the effort you put into your landing page can be priceless. Be sure to consult your Streaming provider as to the effort (and cost) required and based on your application.

The landing page can also be used to house multiple events. Always keep this in mind. If you are running a series of events on a specific subject you will want to use the landing page as a base for these events. Your audience will want one page to access your webcasts, whether upcoming or recently completed. And you can use cookies to track your users so they don't need to register separately for each event. If they register for your first webcast on investing in Asian Markets and then go back to watch the on-demand replay of your webcast on Brexit and its Effect on the European Economy, they will only need to register once. When they log in to the second event, instead of new registration information being required and requested the landing page will recognize the returning user and automatically let them know an email is being forwarded to them with the link to the event they wish to view.

Registration

Every webcast event should start with registration. The data that can be obtained through registration is invaluable, and every effort should be made to maximize the data to be retrieved from this.

When I talk to my customers about an upcoming webcast they wish to complete I always start with registration. By creating the registration you are essentially creating a database for future mining and access. The registration database serves as the engine to drive the analytics being captured from your event. Yes, we have some customers that don't want or need registration, but these are very rare circumstances and I strongly urge against this practice. The only argument for not having a robust registration engine is for the anonymity of your participating audience. But, again, this is rare and strongly discouraged by most companies in the industry.

So what can we capture through the registration process? It would probably be easier to ask, what can we *not* capture? Typical registration begins with first name, last name, email address, and organization/company. Those four elements are at the heart of most registration engines in the industry. A truly knowledgeable and up-to-date user of webcasting technology, however, will go way beyond those fields.

Keep in mind, the registration process is how you capture most of the information on your viewing audience. I can't stress that enough. The more information you request during the registration process, the better the information you will obtain through the post-event analytics and reporting. Here are a few of the additional registration fields I've seen for a virtual event:

- Phone number
- City/State
- Geographical location
- Age range
- Household Income
- Industry
- Direct Manager
- Investment Strategy

- College/University   - Major

The data collected will be driven by the application being Streamed. For example, a webcast run by a financial institution as a marketing application to try and attract high net-worth investors may ask about Household Income but probably does not care about your college major. An application Streamed by an HR department as a recruiting tool will be concerned about your college major and may even ask about your GPA.

In addition to canned answers (multiple choice answers such as age range or investment strategy) many registration fields can also be made open-form, requiring the registrant to give specific information ("what interests you the most about this topic?"). Of course, you don't want to discourage your audience by having them fill out 15-20 fields with multiple open-form fields for registration purposes. In my experience customers will be turned off to the event if they have to enter more than six drop-down registration fields and have to answer more than two open-form registration questions. Try not to overwhelm your customer: yes, information capture is paramount, but losing a potential customer because they simply didn't like your registration process should always be taken into account.

White-listing/Black-listing – Security is always a concern when creating the registration for your event. How do you prevent your competitors from joining your public (or private) event? There are several ways to complete this. Probably the most secure way is to make your event by invitation only. This means you must have a registered email address in order to register and attend. A listing of pre-qualified email addresses is submitted to the creator of your event. If you are not on the list, you can't register or attend.

Whitelisting and blacklisting are two additional ways. By whitelisting you are telling the event host that, in order to view the live event, you must have a @company.com email domain. Anyone with that domain can register and view. If you don't have that domain, you cannot view.

But what about someone who registers with a fake email address but the correct domain? Good question! They *will* be able to register, since the email is not checked until the registration process is complete. But once they register, the links to access the live event are emailed to the specified email address in the registration. If the email is fake – regardless of the validity of the domain name – no access links will be made available to the fake email address.

Blacklisting can also aid in your security efforts. By blacklisting domains you can prevent certain parties from even registering for the event. Should a registrant submit her @competitorx.com email address the registration engine will see the domain as blacklisted and deny the registration.

I'm always surprised at how few companies use blacklisting for their registration. I've attended many of my competitors' events, for the purposes of gathering information on the enemy, without being questioned as to my intentions because they didn't blacklist my domain name. Yes, I will occasionally get kicked out of live events for being a 'spy' but this requires the hosts of the event to manually troll through the participants on the event long after the event has started and valuable information has been disseminated.

Reporting and Analytics

Probably the heart of your streaming event is the reporting and analytics capabilities. This is especially true if your event is a marketing piece. The ability to capture data on your audience is paramount to any good marketing department. Social media notwithstanding, the ROI from the analytics gleaned from your registration is invaluable.

As we discussed previously, the registration application forms the heart of the database for your event. When you set up your participant registration you are creating a database that will be used to not only house the registration information but all of the data occurring before, during and after your event goes live.

We already outlined, previously, the data that can be collected before your event – this is the registration engine. But once you capture that and set up your database, your event goes live and participants log into the event, you now have access to these fields, and more:

- Attendees
- Length of visit
- Questions asked quizzes and surveys
- Answers received
- Social Media
- And so much more

- Time of login
- Attention tracking
- Responses to polls,
- Blogging
- Time of exit

As you can see, this data is invaluable. Not everyone who registers will attend the live event. So tracking actual attendees is very important. Once your event goes live and participants start to join, how engaged are they? Are they submitting questions to the presenter? Are they responding to polls? If you launch an attention tracker – a subroutine that simply asks of your audience, "are you paying attention?" – do they remember to respond that they are, in fact paying attention? How long did they stay tuned in to the live event? Did they Tweet or post to social media (LinkedIn, Facebook) while viewing the live event?

All of this information is made available to you within a short time after the end of the live event through the Streaming reporting portal. All true streaming applications will have this portal and available for you to access. Check with your service provider to determine when and how this portal is available to you.

Regardless if you access and download the analytics yourself or they are emailed to you post-event, you now have a plethora of information on your audience. How you use them is up to you: if you are running an internal town hall for your CEO you can determine exactly how many of the employees tuned in (and stayed tuned in!) to your CEO's video. If you are running a marketing campaign for a financial institution trying to attract high net-worth investors, you can quickly determine how many high net-worth investors participated, where they were located, and how much they participated in your presentation.

And these analytics aren't just limited to your live broadcast. They are available for on-demand viewing, as well. Typically, if you invite 1,000 participants to your marketing webcast, historically you will get 100-200 participants to respond and register. Of those who register, you typically get 50-60% to actually show up for the live event. Some marketing and PR firms will send out 10,000 emails just to get 100-200 participants for the live event. But part of the beauty of the webcast event is that the live event can be edited to remove any dead air time and trim off the first and last moments of silence, then repurposed and re-launched as an on-demand webcast using the same registration page. The participants have the same capabilities to participate in polls, ask questions, download assets, etc., as the live audience (posting a question during an on-demand event will trigger an email to the event host letting her/him know the question was asked during the on-demand replay session). As such, you as the owner of the event can get timed reports showing all of the activity during your on-demand replay. You can track these reports by date, showing you how popular your event was as it ages. Again, the data obtained from both the live and on-demand reporting analytics are invaluable. Work with the project manager of your streaming provider to maximize the return on investment you need for your webcasting event.

e-Learning

On-demand (e-learning) courses have become wildly popular over the past ten years, and Content Streaming plays right into that arena. Educators have the ability to create on-line courses for anything and everything imaginable. The e-learning course is simply an on-demand webcast with advanced registration features and the ability to include grading through the use of quizzes and assessments.

There really is no limit to the educational content available. And courses can either be live or on-demand. A Live event is simply a mass learning exercise where the subject matter expert (SME) gives a lecture to her or his live audience. This can, of course, be archived and viewed as an on-demand replay.

The most common type of e-learning application is the on-demand course. Using advanced registration the content creator can pre-record the session – either with video or audio only – then add in such features as quizzing, pass/fail, and grading.

Of course, the purpose of the e-learning course is to impart wisdom on your audience and subsequently evaluate the trainee. This can be accomplished in several ways:

- Course Completion: the student is 'graded' by whether or not he or she views the entire content of the session. That's it. The webcast simply records the log-in time and log-off time of the student to determine if the entire course was viewed. While simplistic, this can be extremely useful for such applications as HR training, employee benefits, etc.
- Pass/Fail: the student is required to pass an end-of-session exam in order to receive a

passing grade. The benchmark for passing is predetermined by the creator (e.g., 80% correct) as well as the exam. The student can be given the option of skipping the course and jumping straight to the exam, and the creator has the option of allowing the student to re-take the exam without running through the course again. These are all options that are predetermined when developing the course. Examples of these types of e-learning are Ethics Training (sexual harassment), Legal certifications, etc. Once the student passes the exam their score is recorded and the option of printing a certificate is provided.

- Periodic Testing and Quizzing: this type of course is the most intensive. The student views the training for a pre-determined period of time (as set by the course instructor). At the conclusion of that time period a quiz pops up that has to be taken by the student in order to advance in the course. To make it even more complex, the creator may decide that, should the student not pass the quiz, the course will revert to the last section covered to review the material on the quiz and the student is given a new chance to pass the quiz. This is optional, of course. But it is the most intensive way of ensuring the student comprehends and ingests the material. An end-of-course test with certificate is still available, though for this type of e-learning would be redundant.

All of the types of e-learning outlined above rely heavily on both registration and reporting. The registration becomes the key to establishing the database for the particular student, so grading, advancement, etc., can all be tracked. Any and all information gained from the actual session is tied to the database and available in a report module.

Once you have established that e-learning is the way to the future (and who wouldn't?), you can keep your students engaged by creating a

Virtual Learning Environment (VLE). This is simply setting up a series of courses for your students using a landing page and advanced reporting features to track and monitor your student population. Your VLE can be segregated to set aside courses specific to a department (think Customer Service), restricted to specific team members (think Sales Training), or open to the general population (HR, on-boarding, etc.). You can even create a learning path for students where certain courses are required with time deadlines to complete.

Once a course is complete it is removed from the student course load. However, you can always bring it back (repeated learning) should you require the course to be retaken periodically. Students should always have the option of reviewing older courses already completed, so I recommend never taking a course off-line while the content is still relevant.

Finally, to add an element of competition into your course structure, add gamification. Gamification is simply a public scoring for each student that is updated as a course is passed (or not…). Virtual badges can be awarded to students based on their score level. These badges can be virtually displayed for each student throughout the environment or even added to email account settings to automatically be displayed and updated. This provides a spirit of competition between peers as they advance throughout their specific e-learning track. This can also be incorporated into a Virtual Environment (more on that later). I strongly recommend you make learning fun and interesting for your students. Too often I've seen stodgy, on-line courses that are either too difficult to navigate, too boring, or just not the correct medium for the audience. There are lots of on-line tutorials available – and many e-learning vendors – you can use to create your

Virtual Learning Environment using a streaming application. Enjoy!

Virtual Learning Environment Example:

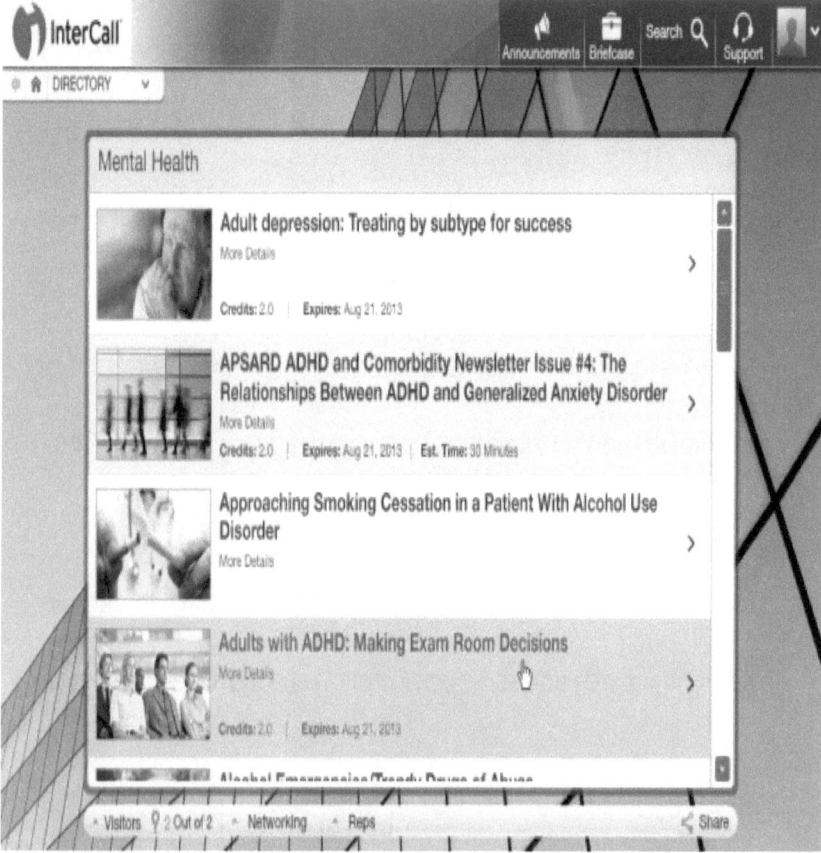

Course Details Example:

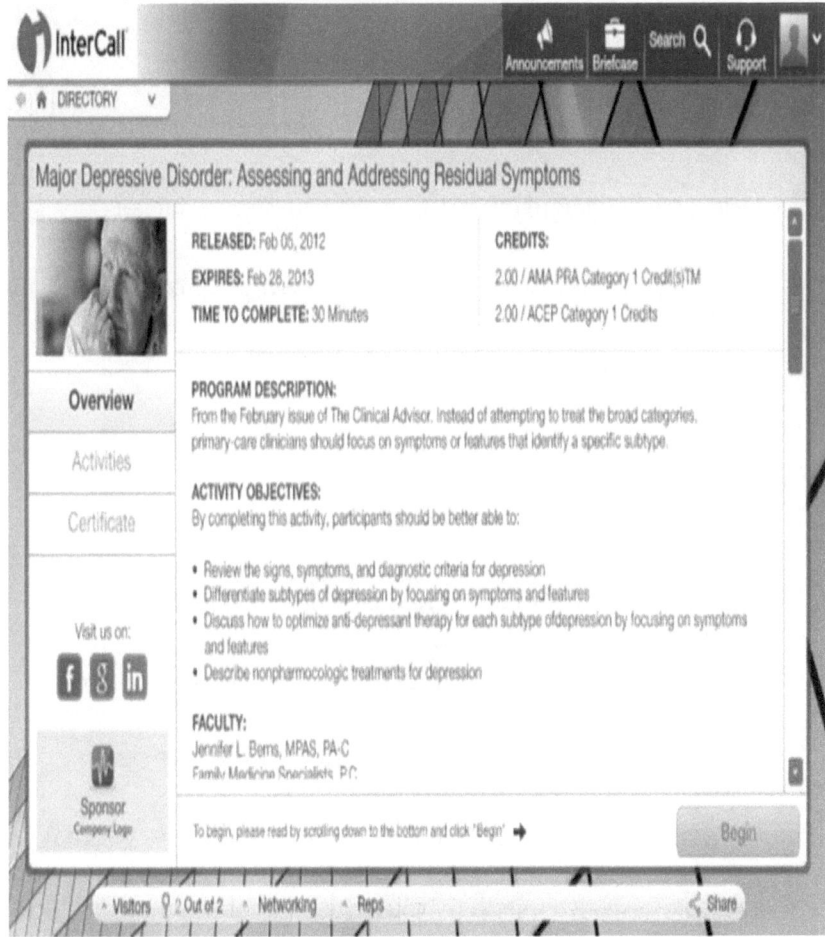

Virtual Environments

Virtual Environments, also known as VECs (Virtual Engagement Campus) have been around for twenty years but really came into vogue with the recession of 2008. The idea behind the VEC is to create a virtual meeting area for employees and customers to interact without having to physically meet or travel. The travel restrictions that came into play in 2008 created an immediate demand for these virtual environments because of cost. A virtual environment can run $60,000 for a full deployment across the enterprise. While this may seem pricy, it pales in comparison to having to fly the entire workforce across the country for a training session.

The way the Virtual Environment works is to emulate a live, on-site experience. The solution is fully customizable, typically taking several months of lead-time to create effectively. The VEC was originally created to replicate a trade show. The VEC can be set up with a registration hall, an exposition center, individual display booths, breakout rooms, a library, and even a theater to stream live and on-demand webcasts.

The Virtual Environment is modeled on the original webcasting application. Just like a live stream, every bit of information is tied to the registration: only the VEC takes the registration a bit farther. The VEC registration will include First Name, Last name, Company, email address, and other variable elements (geography, phone number, company vertical, etc.) it will also include a Brief Case for downloading and off-line storage of assets (more on this shortly). And just like the registration for our streaming application the database records questions posed and answers received while the participant is inside the VEC.

Let's go through some of the typical elements of a Virtual Environment:

Registration Hall – This is where the participants typically enter the VEC. They have previously registered, having filled out all pertinent, required information on the landing page in order to enter the Environment and create the participant's data record. The Registration Hall is typically not manned by a virtual live presence from the VEC creator. However, many customers use an Avatar or pre-recorded greeting to welcome their guests into the Registration Hall and the VEC. The VEC creator simply pre-records an employee giving an opening statement about their Environment: welcome, here's why we're in the VEC, here's what you can see, here's what to do if you have questions, here's how to navigate, etc.

The Registration Hall also serves as the navigation point to the rest of the Environment. From here, the participant has the option of exploring the other customized rooms throughout the VEC. Typically, for the trade show application, the next area to be explored is the Exposition Hall or showroom floor.

Exhibition Hall – This is the heart of the virtual environment. The Exposition Hall is just what it seems: the heart of the convention center where everyone goes during a trade show to explore, meet new people and get demos on new products. Fully customizable, the

Exposition Hall can be outfitted with booths, just like a physical trade show. Participants can interact with each other while in the Exhibition Hall or simply move on to a booth or other section of the VEC. Typically, participants don't spend much time in the Exhibition Hall other than to explore the various booths awaiting them inside.

Booths – Booths are just that: a virtual subset of the Exhibition Hall where participants can get specific information on a company, a product, or almost anything. The booth is where you will house your collateral. You create the booth for a specific function: to draw in your audience to view specifics about your company or products. Documentation is stored here as well as videos or even webcasts. The participant has the ability to download collateral and store in their virtual briefcase for saving to their hard-drive and future download.

The booth – unlike most of the other areas of the Environment – typically is manned by a virtual presence of the hosting company. In other words, a booth attendant is virtually created to interact with the booth guests in real time, answering questions, demoing product, and spurring interest in the booth assets for those attending the booth. You can even host links to cloud demos from the booth; the only downside is that once the participant accesses the link they are taken outside of the VEC. But everything done inside the booth – including access to outside links – is recorded on the data record of the participant and the database is updated.

Theater – The Theater is developed for live events inside the Environment. These are typically a webcast or live stream by the VEC creator. For an Environment set up as a trade show and for a full day, live events by the Conference Host or Subject-Matter Experts are scheduled in the Theater throughout the day. Periodic notifications of these live events are broadcast to all throughout the VEC so participants are made aware of these live events. And, just like a stand-alone Webcast, the participant registers for the live event and all information is recorded to the database.

Library – The Library is a separate room for participants to go for general information provided by the VEC creator. Just like a physical library, the participants are given the ability to download and store whitepapers, collateral, videos, etc., and store these in their briefcase for later viewing. While the collateral stored in the various booths are usually made specific to the theme of the booth, the content stored in the library is going to be of a more general variety, including links to corporate information, investor relations collateral, HR information, or even links to HR and employment opportunities.

Breakout Rooms – The Breakout room is a non-specific area of the VEC designed for your customers to interact without necessarily being overwhelmed by customers or the lure of collateral. It's just a space where your participants can go to meet and virtually chat with each other. Typically the VEC creator will set up a blogging application in the Breakout Room with generic discussion topics so your customers can not only interact with each other but share ideas that can be used by your company to gauge the interest in topics within and outside of your VEC. Additionally, the VEC creator will load an MP4 video file into the Breakout room, running the video on a loop to keep the audience engaged while in the breakout room. This video usually is a 30-60 second advertisement for your firm, though it can be almost anything that you think would pique the interest of your audience.

The Trade Show format is just one example of the usage of a VEC. In the last ten years or so there has been a greater demand to use the Virtual Environment for training sessions (internal VECs for mass training of your enterprise, either live or on-demand) or even career fairs. These are extremely popular for college seniors. Instead of having to send the corporate recruiters on-site to each and every university, a virtual career fair can be set up to allow Seniors to visit and partake in the career fair without leaving their dorm rooms. Recruiters love this, as well, because they can reach a larger audience and interact with anyone and everyone inside the VEC. Instead of the Exhibition Hall being set up for a trade show, it is set up to showcase the various career fields available from a company. Booths are set up to meet and interact personally with recruiters and HR staff and for specific areas of academic study. Instead of an advertisement video being continually looped within the Breakout Room a video is created and run on a continuous loop that shows what the attendees can expect during their first 100 days as an employee at your company.

Think of the VEC as Disneyworld. The customization of the VEC is the key to success. Just like Disneyworld you can set up different realms within your environment. Instead of the Magic Kingdom, EPCOT, and Animal Kingdom, you create Partner Training, Customer Training, and Employee Training realms. And with the registration feature of the VEC you can restrict access to each venue based on the level of registration provided by the participants (customer, partner, employee, contractor, etc.).

The abilities of the VEC are almost unlimited. And the power of the database and data records you create can be invaluable to your company for customer intelligence, competitor analysis, or employee training. Unfortunately, the VEC has fallen out of favor over the last few years as the economy has expanded and companies are allowing more and more physical travel. Still, for large-scale training and information sharing for your employees and customers the VEC is a proven, economically savvy way of communicating in the 21st Century.

To follow are some screenshots from Virtual Environments. This should give you some idea of the power and customization of this type of application:

Welcome Center example:

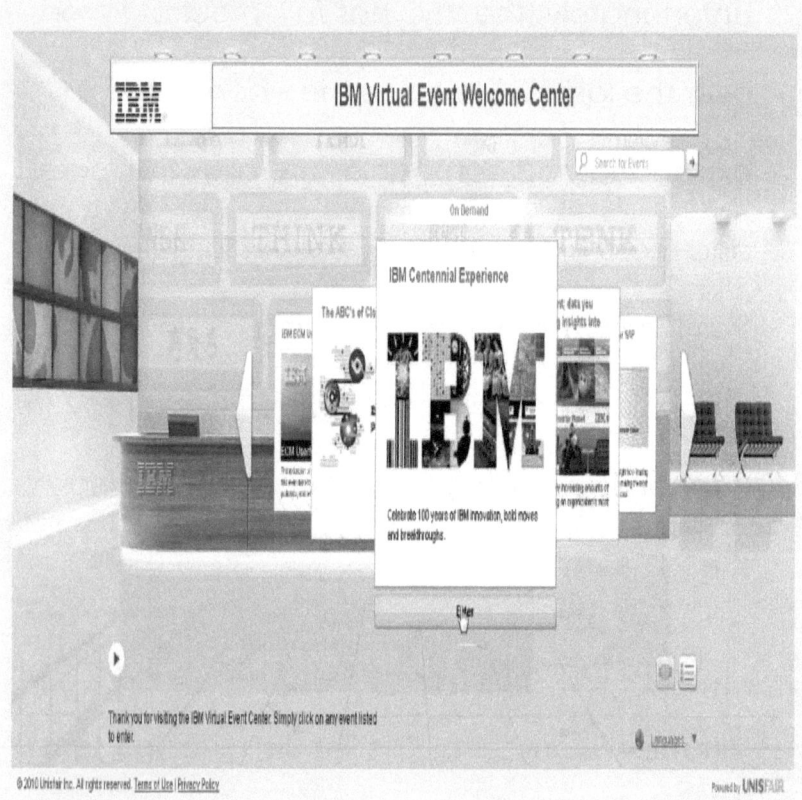

Briefing Center with Talking Head example:

Booth Example #1:

Booth Example #2:

Conference Hall Example:

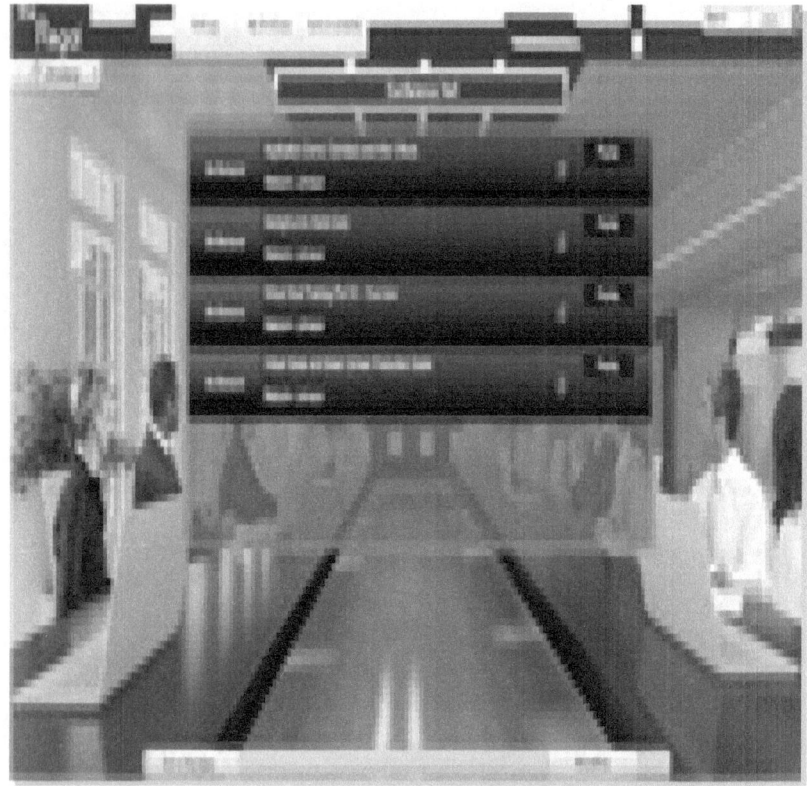

(Note the courses selection are presented as Webcast/Streaming options)

Virtual Campus example:

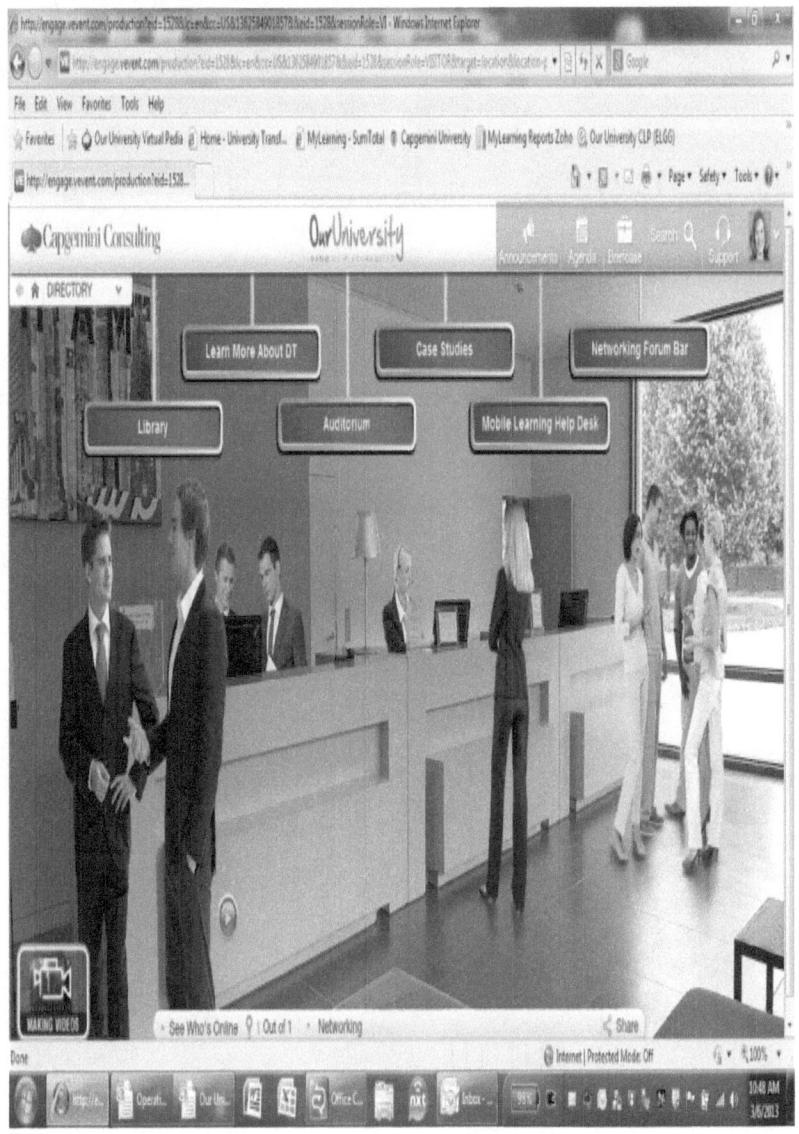

Registration/Landing Page:

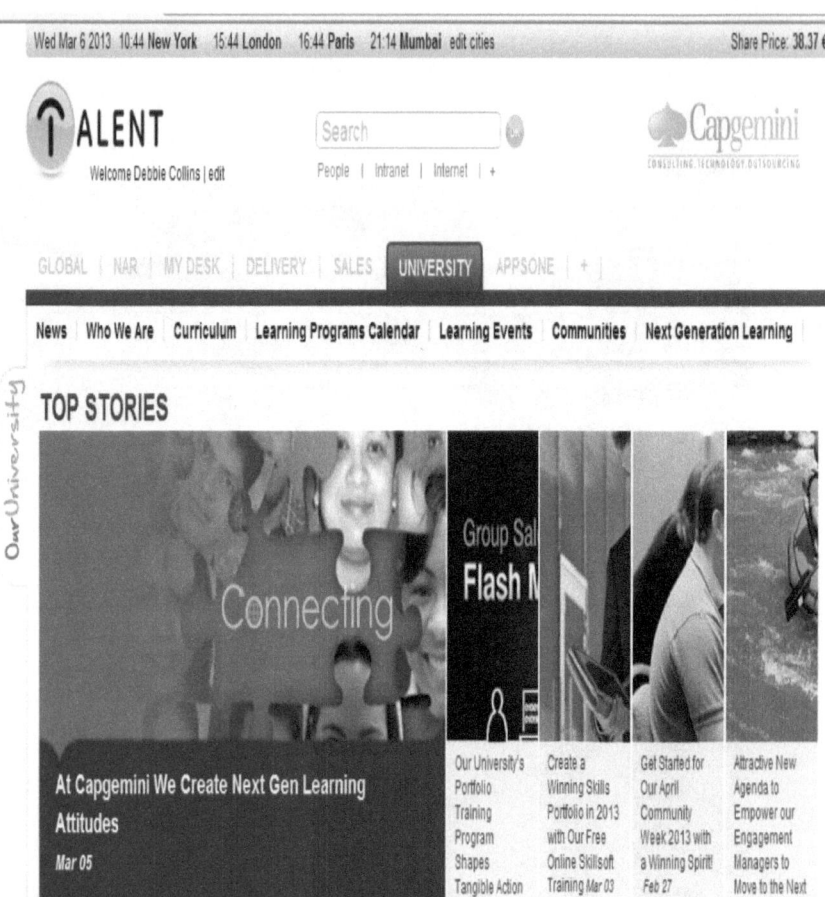

Networking Lounge example:

Exhibition Hall example:

The Future of Streaming

So we've talked all about the past and present in regards to Streaming, Webcasting, Webinars, and Virtual Environments. But what does the future hold? If Content Streaming has been around for 20 years how much more can be done? What is on the horizon that will aid me and my firm for the next 24-36 months???

Great questions!!!

The future of Content Streaming revolves around two thoughts: keeping your audience engaged and interested in the presentation, and reducing the cost of this engagement.

Let's go over where, how and when these two thoughts will be addressed.

...and the beauty here is that these thoughts are being addressed now. You won't have to wait 12-24 months to implement these unique assets of Content Streaming.

One of the biggest issues in Streaming to come along since 2018 is security; specifically, GDPR. GDPR stands for General Data Protection Regulation. While this has been mandated for the European Union, it is just as much a concern in North America, though the US has yet to formalize it. What GDPR does is to provide assurance that any data collected will not be used without the content owner's permission. Almost every company we've dealt with in the past 12 months has required us to show GDPR compliance. This is not a major undertaking; however, to do business with any EU entity you must prove your company and solutions are GDPR compliant.

Security will continue to be a major concern for both public and private entities as the US and other countries are dragged kicking and screaming into the cyber world of the 2st century. We touched upon this in our discussion of the eCDN (above), and as the battlefield of the next 100 years moves to the Cloud the need for a secure Content Streaming service will only grow.

Beyond security, here are some other features of Content Streaming that will emerge over the next 12-24 months.

OTT

OTT stands for Over-the-Top, and is the acronym for on-demand streaming services like Amazon Firestick or Roku. This type of streaming has been around for a few years now, threatening to do away with standard broadcast television. But it is NOT Content Streaming (yet...). Services like Amazon and

Netflix offer these services for streaming on-demand video, and they are truly revolutionary, but we won't spend time on these as they are currently video streaming services and not Content Streaming services. These services will continue to evolve over the next few years as the technology advances, however.

Perpetual Video

Just like OTT, perpetual video is coming to a business near you. Much like the old days of closed-circuit television, Perpetual Video allows you to stream video continuously inside your business's VPN. Companies like Kollective, Kaltura, and Qumu offer these types of services for looping video by loading files into the Network and constantly streaming these videos 24x7x365. The benefits of these types of services are myriad: advanced security, user-generated-content, training, and even secure, top-secret content for specific departments can be run on these solutions. This service tends to be expensive: an enterprise-wide secure on-demand video delivery service with authority levels and multiple channels can run hundreds of thousands of dollars per year. But this solution is not far away, and soon every large enterprise will have a Perpetual Video solution as part of its cyber infrastructure.

Video e-mail

Video e-mail, or v-mail, is already here, but it is slow to be adopted. While everyone now uses webcams when on a live meeting, we still see very few true video emails being used in the corporation. Some leading edge companies get it: one large player in the enterprise has their CEO sending out daily morning updates via video email. Each employee receives an email with an MP4 every morning with the results of the previous day and thoughts for the coming day. Typically, this is no more than 2-3 minutes, but rumor has it it's very effective.

To most of you, this is probably not revolutionary, but as I've pointed out it still has not been widely adopted. Like Perpetual Video, though, it's coming. We are lazy by nature: we would much rather watch a video than read an email. And studies have shown not only are video emails more likely to be opened, they are 4-5 times more effective than standard emails. Just put the word VIDEO in the subject of your next email, and see how many more people open it. Magic!

Video Snippets

Think of Video Snippets like movie trailers: short bursts of content to entice the viewer to learn more about your product, solution or service. Video snippets are becoming more and more popular as a PR tool. We're seeing an upturn in demand for Video Snippets for IR events. Video Snippets are a great way to spruce up your Investor Relations website. Tease your investors and potential investors with these Snippets showing your solutions installed and running, your services being provided to your customers, or even a boardroom meeting video.

These Video Snippets are typically launched as pop-ups. In fact, they're generated much like the pop-up ads you get when you log into any commercial website. Instead of a pop-up coupon or the Customer Service Robot, you get a video Snippet to lure you further into the site. Very good at enticing your customers, and they can be extremely cost-effective: a 30-second Video Snippet can be completed for under $1,000, but the ROI will come across at 20x-30x or more. They are also extremely easy to monitor and edit. Once the Video Snippet reaches its end of life you simply remove it from the queue, then create and upload a new one. Again, Video Snippets are extremely effective for all sorts of marketing; from PR to product placement.

Embedded Video

Embedded Video works much like Video Snippets, but these tend to be much more detailed and extensive. Use Embedded Video to spruce up any website. These videos can be used for advertising, marketing, and even training. Embedded Video can be a flat MP4 file (on-demand streaming video) or an on-demand Webcast. Obviously – and with personal bias included – the on-demand Webcast provides a much more effective means of communication because it not only has video but can include various types of content (see previous discussions on Content Streaming).

Tailor your embedded videos to the application you are working with. Use embedded videos for internal or external customers. We'll talk about this more in an upcoming section, but the three primary areas that most benefit from Content Streaming are Marketing, Training, and Corporate Communications. Use training videos embedded in your Intranet for internal training. Use marketing and product/solutions videos on your external website to show your external customers the benefits provided by your company. And use Embedded Video on your IR website to prove to your investors your company is not only moving in the right direction but has a 3-5 year plan for continued growth. The possibilities are almost unlimited.

Video Press Releases

These are becoming more popular and will continue to grow. In fact, the days of written press releases are numbered. We are much more engaged by video than the written word, and we're much more likely to download a video of the Chairman of the

Board talking about profitability than we are to view a whitepaper talking about business opportunities with the EU post-Brexit.

Corporate Communications and Marketing are leading the way in this arena. Video Press Releases can be expensive, however. A two-camera shoot with paid actors, voice-over, closed-captioning and custom content can run upwards of $50,000. However, a good, savvy CorpComm group can use the in-house video conferencing unit and/or a webcam to create a crisp, effective Video Press Release for under $5,000.

Adaptive Bit Rate

Adaptive Bit Rate (ABR) has been around for a few years, but will become mainstream over the next 12-24 months. Not all enterprises can afford an eCDN, so IT departments will rely more and more on ABR. ABR is a technology that allows end users to control the amount of bandwidth coming into their work station. A Streaming Solution equipped with ABR will auto-detect the amount of bandwidth available on a specific end-user's work station and adapt the band width to meet the needs and availability on the work station. If HD quality video is being streamed, taking up 800k in bandwidth, ABR will proactively work to change the stream to fit the bandwidth available. If only 300k of bandwidth is available, the solution will 'dumb-down' the stream to push the video through in standard definition instead of hi-def. If only 50k of bandwidth is available, ABR will take down the stream to an audio-only stream instead of video. This eliminates the need for massive amount of bandwidth for hi-def video streaming and prevents buffering or even video outage. But it also limits the viewing experience by the end users. Think of it as the poor-man's version of the eCDN. It can be very useful, and it typically does not add any cost to the Content Streaming application. But, as pointed out, it severely limits the content available to the end user.

Mobile Device Go-Live

For most of the history of Content Streaming, and in order to create and start an event, the host had to plan everything hours, days or weeks in advance. To this day most live Streaming events are planned, developed and hosted by personnel in the vendors' Streaming department. But self-service Webcasting is becoming more common (though, as of this writing, most customers still prefer the white-glove service offered by vendors to ensure the Streaming event goes off without a hitch). Streaming through mobile devices such as iPads, iPhones and Android devices has been around for several years (see HTML5, above), but the ability to spontaneously launch and Stream an event from a mobile device has been extremely limited. Now, with Mobile Device Go-Live, all you need is access to the Internet and an email list and you can launch live events quickly and effectively. HR departments can launch mass training applications within minutes by accessing the Enterprise Active Directory (a list of current, accurate employee names and email addresses) and the Streaming app on their mobile device. Extremely efficient and effective!

Multi-SAML/Multi-IDP

Here is the definition of SAML and IDP:

Security Assertion Markup Language (SAML) is an open standard for exchanging authentication and authorization data between parties, in particular, between an Identity Provider (IDP) and Service Provider (SP).

SAML works with SSO (Single-Sign-On) to create a seamless registration and authentication experience for the end user.

SSO and SAML have been integrated into Content Streaming for several years now. By implementing SAML and SSO the host of a series of events can require the participant to only register one time for that series. SAML allows the authentication of the end user, assuring the hos that the end-user is a real entity and not some Bot trying to hack into the event. SAML assures the security not only of the end user but the entire user experience. By implementing SSO, the authenticated end user can access one or hundreds of events on the host platform and eliminate the need to sign in and re-register every time she or he wishes to watch a live or on-demand event.

This is especially important for marketing initiatives. The last thing you want to put your customer through is to have to log in and register every time they wish to view one of your video events. With SSO and SAML enabled you have the assurance that the user is real, and the user has the assurance that they only need to register one time. Very convenient. It also prevents hackers from accessing your network or event simply by loading in the correct passwords.

Now, with multi-SAML/multi-IDP enabled, you bring the whole world of Content Streaming into your end user's world, safely, securely, and effortlessly. Multi-SAML allows for multiple authentications to occur simultaneously without the end-user experiencing anything unusual. With traditional SAML your end user was authenticated using a single solution provided through the Enterprise. Now with Multi-SAML you security authentication is layered into your network and application proving robust security and affirmation of access from authorized participants only.

The Multi-SAML solution works in congress with multi-IDP. More and more of our applications are coming from multiple providers, so a method of secure access through these multiple IDPs had to be created that was not available through traditional SAML/IDP. The Multi-SAML/multi-IDP solution alleviates this issue by allowing secure authentication and access from multiple IDPs. Simply put, instead of a single SAML record created for a single IDP, with multi-SAML/multi-IDP the authentication process does not care how many authentications are required or how many data providers are engaged. All of this happens during the initial registration attempt, ensuring the security of the user and the event host regardless of access or IDP and without pesky passwords. The SSO process is then put in place as the next step. This allows, again, a seamless, secure access for one or multiple events for the end users and ensures network security for the host.

Spoken Word Search

From the very roots of Streaming, hosts have had the ability to add in closed captioning to live events and transcription to on-demand events. This is nothing new. In fact, while I was working for a GSA vendor providing webcasting services to the Federal Government we were required to provide captioning and transcription services to almost all of our Federal events. This was known as Section 508 compliance: Section 508 compliance refers a section of the United States Workforce Rehabilitation Act mandating that all electronic and information technology developed, procured, maintained, or used by the Federal Government be accessible to people with disabilities. Simple enough, but it was vital to those with hearing loss.

It also provided an additional application for searching for on-demand events through the Internet. With transcription enabled, web surfers could now search for content by key words without knowing the specific topic or title of the webcast. Searches for Global Warming or Tea Party initiatives will yield thousands of results through Google; many of them on-demand Webcasts.

The issue, however, is that the key word would either have to be in the title of the event or listed in the transcription of the webcast. But only a very small portion of on-demand webcasts available on the Internet have transcription. This is where Spoken Word Search will come into play. With advanced search features and software solutions enabled surfers will have the ability to search non-transcribed webcasts on the Internet through Spoken-Word Search. The program will be smart enough through speech recognition to identify key words through the audio signal of the spoken word. This will open up millions of documents to this search technique and provide a much more robust, content-rich search.

Bandwidth Mitigation

Currently, there are only two options available to limit the amount of bandwidth required for Content Streaming applications (assuming you are using a Unicast Streaming platform). The first is the eCDN. As we discussed previously, the eCDN limits the amount of bandwidth required for all devices throughout your network to one single point of entry. It's a terrific technology that gives you HD video capabilities throughout your network without the shimmying, buffering and drops traditionally associated with streaming video. It does have its draw-backs, however. Whenever you use your eCDN to stream you will experience a significant lag time between broadcast and signal receipt. In other words, the message from the speaker of record will take 30-45 seconds (or more!) to reach the end user. And this is not dependent on the size of the network. Every endpoint on the eCDN will experience this lag. The end user will not notice it, however. But the speaker trying to keep his or her audience engaged may be affected because it may take up to a full minute for users to respond to polls, or questions submitted may be significantly behind the actual dialogue being presented by the speaker.

The other method we discussed, above, is Adaptive Bit Rate. This is most effective for external Stream events where the presenter has no control over the bandwidth availability of the end user. Unlike the eCDN application, the delay in the broadcast is typically less than five seconds. The downside, as we've already discussed, is that video may be downgraded or simply unavailable for the end user on a given broadcast.

It's only a matter of time before chip makers like Intel or AMD to catch up to the bandwidth requirements of video applications. The surge in video usage has been astounding (as I'm sure you've already realized). I predict in the next 5-7 years the chip makers will be able to provide enough bandwidth to make the eCDN and even ABR obsolete technologies. Price to install a network capable of complex video applications will fall dramatically, and video will be everywhere. This evolution in Streaming will be upon us before we know it. Will we be ready for it?!

Multi-video streams

Traditionally, a webcast could only stream live one video presenter at a time. But with solution advances and vendors like Inxpo multiple videos can be streamed simultaneously. Vendors like BlueJeans have been doing this for several years (though they have yet to master Content Streaming as of this writing). Now you have the ability to house roundtable discussions with multiple video inputs without the need for swapping out the Presenters each and every time. And with advanced controls, you can swap in speakers easily without disruption to the flow of your event all while keeping your audience engaged and responsive.

360 Video

360 Video has been around for some time, but the costs have always been prohibitive. New technology has brought the price-point down to where this is becoming more affordable. However, the limitations of the viewing platform make this more of a nice-to-have rather than a must-have. Still, 360 Video can be useful especially for town hall applications where it is ideal to have both the speakers and the audience on screen at the

same time. The price points for practical viewing applications will keep this technology as more of a fad than a practical use for many years to come.

The Harmonic Convergence...

In the not-too-distant future you will see the convergence of all things Streaming into one neat, hosted site that will contain all the elements in the current Streaming toolkit. From one website or landing page you will be able to see all your streaming applications:

- PR
- IR
- Internal Content Streaming
- External Events
- CorporateTube/Portal Applications

...and all the metrics that go along with these. You will be able to see in one snapshot just how well each is (or isn't...) performing. You'll be able to quickly get an ROI on the marketing piece you sent out to your High-Net-Worth investors, get a listing of everyone in your Enterprise that has taken your latest product training, see how your PR campaign is performing in EMEA, and observe the results of your latest Quarterly Report as viewed by your investor community.

Companies such as West DMS are working on this convergence right now. It will come out as a toolbox that you can customize to give you the exact information you require for daily, weekly or quarterly snapshots of just how well your digital Content Streaming applications are doing. Stay tuned. This is exciting!

Practical Uses

We've examined the past, present and future of Content Streaming. Now let's talk about some practical applications for this service. After all, technology is awesome, but it means little if we don't know how to use it for practical applications and improvement in our business processes.

There are three areas or sweet spots for Content Streaming Technology.

- o Corporate Communications: the everyday communication on our processes and procedures between and inside our enterprise

- Marketing: Communicating our message to our customers
- Training: Continuous improvement of processes, procedures and services to our internal and external customers

Let's take a look at practical applications of Content Streaming in these three areas.

Corporate Communications

Content Streaming for use by CorpComm is probably the oldest form of use for this technology. Getting your voice heard by management, your team members and peers, and your staff is vital in the business world. To follow are some applications for Content Streaming you may not be considering:

R&D

With today's virtual work force it is becoming more and more common to have a staff made up of off-site (remote) workers. Content Streaming is ideal for this situation. As we pointed out at the beginning of this book Content Streaming is a geographically agnostic technology. It works anywhere and for anyone with an Internet browser. R&D

projects are ideal for this as you can not only share content across the world and across departments, ideas can be easily shared with secure transmission. Use a forum application to set up a continuous blog (or several blogs!) on a new idea under development. Live stream the research team as they present their latest findings through video and PowerPoint while the Development staff weighs in with opinions and facts. You can keep this completely internal to your company by employing the necessary security such as white-listing the participants (limiting access to specific email addresses). Record the entire presentation then set up a landing page to house all of the streamed sessions for a specific project. This creates a historical record that can easily be used for reference by the R&D team at anytime, anywhere. The landing page can double as a secure site with access only allowed by invitation.

Sales/Product Launches

I really like this as an untapped usage of Content Streaming. Similar to the R&D application, above, you can use Content Streaming for introducing a new product or solution to your sales force. Record a video presentation of your newest product being used in the field. This becomes B-roll footage to be used during the live event. After the live introduction on the Webcast, load the B-roll video into the application and play it for your sales staff. While the video is playing a forum feature allows your sales staff to trade ideas and comment on the usage of the new technology or service. Instead of throwing the product over the fence to the sales force you are now giving them a practical, real-world look at how the product or service is to be used by their customers. AND, you are allowing them to give feedback on their thoughts or ideas. It also gives the executive team a first look at how the sales force will truly perceive this new product release.

We had a large cosmetics customer do just this for their sales staff. They had announced, internally, a new line of lipstick applications set to be released into the market. Before the release, however, they made a 15-minute film of the new products being used by consumers. They showed how real customers were using and reacting to the new products; they did not just make a glitzy commercial and present that to the sales force. The executive team and the R&D staff then invited the sales force for an internal product release, along with selected members of the marketing team. The live webcast began, and shortly after introductions were made and expectations were set the host loaded and launched the b-roll of the product being used by customers. The sales staff was invited to log on to the forum application that was housed in the social media section of the webcast. They were then asked to express their thoughts about the new product and its uses. After the conclusion of the event we were told by the customer how invaluable this feature served to provide real and accurate feedback from the sales staff not only to R&D but to the Marketing department. Our customer has gone on to use this custom application successfully many times since first launching. We have been told it has shortened the ramp-up required by the sales force to get behind new products as well as give new insights to the marketing team when positioning their ads to their customers.

This type of application for Content Streaming is very rare, however. The general business population has just not caught on to how valuable this type of feedback can be. Yes, they are definitely in tune with the impact social media can have (more on that shortly), but this type of internal messaging has not gotten a great deal of usage. But I am optimistic it will gain new life as we move into the future of Content Streaming applications.

Investor Relations

For much of the past twenty years – since Streaming entered as a practical communications method – Investor Relations (IR) events were as simple as an audio-only stream. The speakers would give a presentation on quarterly earnings and that's about it. No questions; no comments from the audience; not even a PowerPoint slide deck.

One-way communication at its best and simplest.

But times are changing. More and more, IR events are streaming with PowerPoint files so investors can visualize results, not just hear them. Traditionally, the Board was reluctant to share results live with the investors, but we have seen a change in thought here so that showing results in real time are becoming more important to information dissemination. With the onset of video presentations, we are even seeing the Board give a video IR presentation. Now you can not only see results posted but view the presenters as they post results live. Most boards are still very reluctant to do this, but we see this moving more and more into the mainstream of IR events.

Marketing

Just like Investor Relations sited above, Marketing is an ideal space for Content Streaming. In fact, since this application is launched outside your network, Marketing applications for Content Streaming are some of its oldest uses. Going back to the days of on-demand only streaming (see previous history of Content Streaming) companies used this application to get information into their customer's hands. Big Pharma and Associations were some of the very first users of this technology. We had customers like National Geographic creating on-line content to get their readers excited about the space they owned. Pharma used on-demand Content Streaming to drum up support for the latest drugs and treatments developed. Very effective!

But now, with live streaming becoming more and more prevalent, customers are demanding live interaction with information providers. To follow are some examples of Content Streaming for Marketing applications.

Ask-the-Expert

Ask-the-Expert Marketing programs using Content Streaming have been around for years. However, with the prevalence of video, this is becoming more economical and much easier. And, with advanced analytics available from most Streaming engines, you can have a very positive ROI experience.

A classic example is the Association that wants to attract new members to its cause (or re-invigorate the existing base of support!). Use Content Streaming to shore up a live video of a Subject Matter Expert (SME). This will allow you to not only stream the live video of your SME but get valuable content into the hands of your viewers. This could be a PowerPoint file or even an on-demand video that can be downloaded and saved by your viewing audience.

Financial institutions do this to attract new investors. Give a live Webcast of a Financial Planner discussing investment strategies for the short-term, or broadcast a Retirement Specialist focusing on baby-boomer retirement strategies (or any other generation, for that matter). Use content to add punch to the speech by including PowerPoint slides depicting long-term growth, short-term gains, and/or strategies for passing on your estate to your heirs. All extremely effective ways of communicating with and gaining information on your target audience.

This is where the power of analytics comes to the forefront. You can create a registration engine that captures all of the pertinent information on your audience: age, geography, level of income, investment risk assessment, health history, etc., etc. The amount and quality of information you can collect is almost limitless. And by blasting out this registration to anyone that may have an interest you are bound to cull a group of participants that will not only be avid viewers of your streamed content but most likely will return for further discussion and information on the topic at hand. And, again, because this is streaming outside of your network you do not need to take bandwidth into consideration when developing your program.

The limits of using Content Streaming for Marketing applications are almost unbounded. Get that content out to your audience, whether through a live stream as outlined above or by posting on-demand videos on sites like LinkedIn, Twitter, etc. But get that content out there!

This also brings in Social Media to the equation. The ability to link Content Streaming to Social Media applications has been around for years, but now, with the continued push for video, this has become even more relevant. Not only can you push your registration through Social Media like Twitter and LinkedIn, but you can link your application – both live and on-demand – to your Social Media channels. Encourage your participants to use their Twitter account to tie in to your live marketing event so your audience can Tweet in real time about the content being shared. Hook LinkedIn to your Marketing event so professionals can share the experience throughout their LinkedIn network. And the same can be done for on-demand applications: encourage your on-demand viewing audiences to share their thoughts on your marketing applications whenever and wherever they view these. This will (naturally!) increase your marketing presence dramatically, and your company – through analytics developed through your registration engine – will have a myriad of information available to you on your participants, all downloaded at your convenience. It is almost overwhelming how much information will become available; it's up to you to decide what information you need to collect, save and disseminate regarding your audience.

PR (Public Relations)

Public Relations is about to explode with the advent of Content Streaming. The old-school days of static PR releases is fast waning. The new ear of video is here. Use Content

Streaming to liven up your boring press releases. Use a landing page to capture your audience and entice them to view the PR piece (assuming that you're not just blasting out an email). Use video snippets to enhance and entice the viewer to read through your press release.

Once the viewer has opened the press release – email or otherwise – you can use Content Streaming to engage the audience and enhance the viewer experience. Use a video of your Chairman or CEO introducing and kicking off your piece. Use your employees in a video clip as they employ your new software or service. Show actual customers putting your product to use.

The convergence of PR and Content Streaming is just now happening, but it is truly an exciting time for PR Professionals to engage the use of video. I've said this before: Video is five times more likely to be viewed (and retained!) than standard written content. And you now have the ability to track this through the use of advanced analytics. You will be able to see who, how and when your audience is engaged in your public relations piece. If you ask for an email address, you can then turn these into leads for your sales team. The reality is that the convergence of Content

Streaming and Public Relations has the power to increase your ROI exponentially.

Training

Using Content Streaming for Training applications is not something new. However, and again with the advent of video, it has taken on a whole new usage. Learning Management Systems (LMS) have been using Content Streaming for some time, but because these are typically behind-the-firewall applications they have been limited to audio-and-PowerPoint only. Now, with the widespread usage of eCDN, Training applications can take on both live and on-demand video to enhance and augment the Training experience.

I believe we will see more and more training move to both live and on-demand usage over the next few years. Users will become more and more confident of using video, whether creating this Training from their office or using a professional studio to enhance the quality. Almost every enterprise now has some sort of training application for their employees. Content Streaming can add a dimension on top of this that was previously unavailable. You now have the power to get training scheduled, to grade, and to ensure your employees are taking training as required by law, when necessary (HIPPA, GDPR, are just two examples).

Solutions for your LMS can offer rich, robust training applications. It's up to you and your staff to determine the appropriate level of interaction needed. Some uses of internal, on-demand training include:

- New Employee Training
- HR (Sexual Harassment, Workplace Conduct, EOE, etc.)
- Legal (Document Retention, Data Use & Storage, etc.)
- R&D (to document processes, Project Management, workflow, etc.)
- And much more

Content Streaming can also be used for live training. We have seen an uptick in the usage of large-scale training sessions for enterprises globally. These 'Training Mash-ups" usually involve a Keynote Speaker giving a presentation to a large (see: global) audience in which high-level information is provided. These Training Mash-ups typically attract tens of thousands of viewers. And with your installed eCDN, you no longer have to worry about the Stream of your Chief Science Officer blanking out because of lack of bandwidth. This is an extremely effective method of getting information into the hands of your work force, quickly and easily (and inexpensively! Imagine the budget needed to fly your Chief Science Officer all over the world to update your R&D staff on the roadmap for the next 36 months vs. doing this large-scale Training Mash-up).

Much of the training you will utilize inside your network will be informal (employee on-boarding, etc.), but there will be a huge demand and requirement for formalized, certifiable training. This is truly a sweet spot for Content Streaming. Many associations use Content Streaming for certification of its members. It's not unusual to get emails in your in-basket touting CE credits for Legal and any other certifiable education application. With

Content Streaming, you can now have accreditation at your fingertips. It is very simple to set up a certificate course with various levels of accountability. Here are some of the practical applications for certification course:

- *Viewership* Simply view the application and gain credit. The participant merely needs to sit through the presentation. No quiz or certification required.
- *Pass/Fail* A quiz is presented at the end of the course and participants are required to pass an exam at the end. Parameters for passing the exam are provided by the course creator.

- *Grading* Participants who have selected and taken a course must take a post-course exam and achieve a certain percentage in order to be awarded a certificate. If they don't pass with the required percentage, they can either be prompted to take the quiz again, or they can be informed that they must review the presentation again and re-take the exam (to be really devious, you can even require the review to be retaken at a future date, instead of immediately after the failing grade is recorded).
- *In-Course quiz* The concept of the In-Course Quiz is fairly new. The idea is that

participants must take periodic quizzes while viewing the presentation. This should occur every few minutes, thereby keeping the participant interested and engaged in the content being delivered. As an example, every three minutes (or 4-5 PowerPoint slides) a quiz pops up on the participant's screen. He/she must answer at least one question posed from the material just viewed. If the quiz is passed, the course continues. If the quiz is failed, the course backs up to a pre-determined point and the material from the quiz is reviewed again. It is then required of the participant to re-take the quiz. It is up to you, the content creator, to determine how many times a participant is allowed to re-take the quiz before he/she bombs out of your course! But this keeps the course participant engaged in the content, and it also ensures the content is being absorbed by the attendee.

There are many more applications for both live and on-demand training. But you can get an idea of the breadth and scope of training available. You are only limited by the requirements imposed on you by your executives (or Legal, or Government), and the content you create and provide to your viewing audience.

And speaking of content, we now come to

the last portion of our book...

Content is King!

With all the emphasis on video and Streaming, it's easy to forget the most important element: Content. Without proper content, you will lose your audience!

So what constitutes great content? That depends a lot on your audience! But the one area you DON'T need to worry is your ability. Anyone can create great content that keeps your audience compelled. To follow are a few simple rules to keep your audience truly engaged in your Digital Media event.

Video

This should go without saying, but video keeps your audience engaged several times over vs. audio or a static presentation. I've seen statistics that video presentations are four times more likely to keep your audience engaged.

Live vs. On-Demand Video

Either is engaging! If you don't feel confident doing a live video, no problem! Create an on-demand video that you can edit to make exceptional. This video can be of anything. It can be you, your team, your company, your customers. Put some effort into outlining what and how you want to present. You'll be surprised how little effort is required to come up with an incredible video.

Keep it Short and To-the-Point

Nothing will turn off your audience faster than a long video that drags. One of the first things your viewers will do when watching your video is look at the length of your video. Ideally, keep it under 5-7 minutes (3-5 is even better!). You can make your case very effectively with a short, intense video. Try it!

Avoid the Talking Head!

Too often I've seen video content where the speaker is simply reading the PowerPoint slides. This is worse – honestly – than no video at all. You will put your audience to sleep very quickly. If possible, walk around while you create your video. The changing background will catch the attention of the viewer and impel them to watch. If you can't walk around, be sure to use hand gestures and facial expressions to impart tone and excitement into you presentation. This may seem silly at first, but it works!

Simu-Live

If you're still unsure of your ability for live video, but you are compelled to create a live event anyway, create a simu-live video. This is simply pre-recording the video, editing to make it complete, then loading it into the live event and streaming. Your audience may or may not know it's pre-recorded, but it won't matter. Once the simu-live video ends, you simply switch to live video. This is commonly done for a town hall where you want to capture and disseminate pertinent information to your enterprise, then take live questions from your on-site or virtual audience. This is extremely effective in creating an engaging solution while keeping the live element for your audience.

PowerPoint and Other Files

Everyone uses PowerPoint slides in their Content Streaming Presentation (well, anyone who wishes to disseminate pertinent information to their audience). This is nothing new. But the trick is to keep your PowerPoint files engaging. Too often I've seen executives put together 30-45 page PowerPoint files for a five-minute presentation. This will lose your audience quickly. A good rule-of-thumb is to keep your slides down to one every 3-5 minutes. Try not to use more than 10-12 slides in total. Start with an introduction slide, then dive right into content. Remember that your audience will be viewing this – most likely – both live and on-demand. So you want to keep your Slides presentation engaging, short, and on point.

Lastly, always finish with...

Questions

ALWAYS finish your presentation leaving your audience with the ability to ask or submit questions. If live or simu-live, this is easy. Your last PowerPoint slide should simply read, "Questions?" This is the queue to your audience to engage with the live speaker (assuming they haven't been engaging through the Streaming platform all along). By leaving time for questions you are inviting your audience to partake in your event.

This is the most engaging application you can add to your Content Streaming event. If a live or simu-live event, simply encourage your audience to submit questions via the platform, then sort and prioritize these questions for the speaker(s) of record. Very easy to do.

If your presentation is on-demand, simply encourage your audience to submit questions through the console. Let them know that all questions will be viewed and answered as appropriate. We discussed this previously, but all Content Streaming applications have an on-demand Q&A that is linked to the email address of the Host or Speaker. This is a great tool that allows for quick response to questions submitted to the Speakers during the on-demand period of your event. The recipient of the question can respond via email to the submitter or, if you remember to capture the participants' phone numbers during the registration process, you can call him or her directly with your answer. Very engaging and very personal!

Conclusion

As I write this, video and Content Streaming has become pandemic in the business world. No longer relegated to home entertainment, advances such as eCDN and Video Portal applications have brought this technology into the mainstream of our business processes. As I stated previously, it's almost impossible to go through the day without watching at least one video while at work, and attending at least one virtual meeting where someone is using video. The price point has come down so much that video is now everywhere (my local jurisdiction has plans to begin mounting cameras on stop signs to nab those who don't stop: that's how cheap it's become).

But video isn't the only element to this phenomenon. As I pointed out in the previous section, without great content, your efforts to stream will be for naught. Take some time to put together a great Content Streaming application, and you will become the go-to person in your company for all things virtual. A great virtual event can help you with:

- Marketing
- Corporate Communications
- Training
- Lead Generation

- Data Mining

...and hundreds of other opportunities to increase your ROI.

You can use Content Streaming for:

- Daily CEO updates to the Enterprise
- Employee On-boarding
- Virtual Recruiting
- Internal Training (HR, Legal)
- External Training (suppliers, customers)
- Product Marketing & Feedback
- Investor Relations
- Public Relations

The list goes on and on. You are only limited by your imagination and the content you create. I hope this book has been valuable as we move into the age of Content Streaming. I truly believe anyone can use these guidelines to create meaningful, engaging content that will delight your audience and keep them attentive to your message.

For more information, follow me on LinkedIn:

https://www.linkedin/in/ScottKutos

Biography

Scott Kutos has been a Senior Leader in the Digital Media Solutions space for more than 15 years. He has been an Executive Leader in Hi-Tech for more than 25 years and currently works for West DMS. As a Sales Leader he has worked to develop and sell Content Streaming Solutions to global enterprises such as State Farm, United Airlines, Wells Fargo, Cargill, American Airlines, Fidelity Advisors, John Deere, Coca-Cola, and Zebra Technologies. Scott currently lives in Bethesda, MD with his wife, Lottie.

A prolific video blogger, you can find his regular video updates on all things Content Streaming at:

https://www.linkedin/in/ScottKutos

www.ingramcontent.com/pod-product-compliance
Lightning Source LLC
Chambersburg PA
CBHW031619210526
45464CB00004B/1659